Crappy Advice
FOR A
Happy Life

Crappy Advice
FOR A
Happy Life

100 Simple Rules on
How NOT to Live Happily Ever After

Kara Lane

Copyright © 2025 by Kara Lane

All rights reserved. No part of this book may be reproduced in any form or by any means without the written permission of the author (ask nicely and I may say OK), except in the case of brief quotations in articles or reviews.

https://www.karalane.com/
The Library of Congress Control Number (LCCN) has been applied for.

Hardcover ISBN 978-1-7339379-5-5
Paperback ISBN 978-1-7339379-3-1
eBook ISBN 978-1-7339379-4-8

Printed in the United States of America
Kara Lane Publishing
Carmel, Indiana

First Edition

This book is dedicated to anyone who's ever been unhappy at any point in their entire life. There aren't many of us, so I hope you'll find some helpful advice in my little guide.

Table of Contents

To Whom It May Concern: 1

Rule 1   Cultivate indifference to things that don't affect you . . . 4
Rule 2   Be impatient when you want something 6
Rule 3   Act on your feelings of jealousy 8
Rule 4   Practice indecisiveness 10
Rule 5   Procrastinate for as long as you can 12
Rule 6   Get results without effort 14
Rule 7   Complain as much as possible 16
Rule 8   Criticize people to make them better 18
Rule 9   Worry incessantly 20
Rule 10 Start fights 22
Rule 11 Don't stand up for others 24
Rule 12 Be as selfish as you can get away with 26
Rule 13 Don't be grateful 28
Rule 14 Blame your problems on other people 30
Rule 15 Talk about what you're going to do, but don't do it 32
Rule 16 Ignore health and wellness data 34
Rule 17 Get upset over petty stuff 36
Rule 18 Ignore the Golden Rule 38
Rule 19 Control other people 40
Rule 20 Let other people control you 42
Rule 21 Believe everything you hear 44
Rule 22 Stay in your comfy zone 46
Rule 23 Curb the impulse to help family and friends 48
Rule 24 Carefully cultivate your image 50
Rule 25 Spend your money as fast as you make it 52

Rule 26	Don't try to figure out what's important to you	54
Rule 27	Overthink everything	56
Rule 28	Plan everything or nothing	58
Rule 29	Try to meet everyone's expectations	60
Rule 30	Be a taker, not a giver	62
Rule 31	Only do what you feel like doing	64
Rule 32	Be a perfectionist	66
Rule 33	Hold extremist political views	68
Rule 34	Take things personally	70
Rule 35	One-up people at every opportunity	72
Rule 36	Act entitled if you had a privileged upbringing	74
Rule 37	Don't be a team player	76
Rule 38	Never ask for help	78
Rule 39	Don't bother with details	80
Rule 40	Seek the approval of others	82
Rule 41	Don't seek excellence	84
Rule 42	Squander your potential	86
Rule 43	Stop learning after you get out of school	88
Rule 44	Never do anything bold	90
Rule 45	Set vague goals	92
Rule 46	Impress people with your intelligence	94
Rule 47	Beware of anything fun or adventurous	96
Rule 48	Hang out with negative people	98
Rule 49	Let others compensate for your disorganization	100
Rule 50	Don't look for humor in life	102
Rule 51	Don't worry about the consequences of your actions	104
Rule 52	Never change, and don't believe others who claim to have changed	106
Rule 53	Monopolize conversations	108
Rule 54	Skip the positive self-talk because words don't matter	110
Rule 55	Express your anger when things don't go your way	112

Rule 56	Never sit still	114
Rule 57	Be judgmental	116
Rule 58	Never apologize	118
Rule 59	Keep doing what's not (yet) working	120
Rule 60	Make excuses every chance you get	122
Rule 61	Don't commit to anyone or anything	124
Rule 62	Be fearful	126
Rule 63	Be skeptical	128
Rule 64	Dwell on the past	130
Rule 65	Only see things from your perspective	132
Rule 66	Never forgive people	134
Rule 67	Beat yourself up when you make a mistake	136
Rule 68	Be a doormat	138
Rule 69	If you grudgingly agree to do something, make sure everyone knows you resent it	140
Rule 70	Avoid persistence	142
Rule 71	Don't stoop to doing menial tasks	144
Rule 72	If you're wealthy and greedy, use your money and power strictly for your benefit	146
Rule 73	If you're able-bodied but lazy, find ways to game the system	148
Rule 74	Don't be authentic	150
Rule 75	Be 100% consistent in your opinions	152
Rule 76	Expect everything to be easy	154
Rule 77	Embrace boredom	156
Rule 78	Avoid stating an opinion if possible	158
Rule 79	Spend all your time on your devices	160
Rule 80	Be oblivious	162
Rule 81	Never do for yourself what you can get others to do for you	164
Rule 82	Do everything yourself	166

Rule 83	Insist that everything be fair	168
Rule 84	Listen to the haters	170
Rule 85	Be an insensitive-sensitive person	172
Rule 86	Credit your success to skill and your failures to bad luck, but credit other people's success to good luck and their failures to their weaknesses	174
Rule 87	Let a lack of knowledge hold you back	176
Rule 88	Don't reflect on your life	178
Rule 89	Speak before you think	180
Rule 90	Don't believe in yourself	182
Rule 91	Maximize your wealth and flaunt it	184
Rule 92	Choose your friends based on their looks, money, achievements, and connections	186
Rule 93	Turn everything into a problem	188
Rule 94	Avoid confrontation	190
Rule 95	Put limitations on yourself	192
Rule 96	Play the victim	194
Rule 97	Constantly compare yourself to others	196
Rule 98	Jump to conclusions	198
Rule 99	Expect other people to make you happy	200
Rule 100	Constantly chase after happiness	202

How'd you do? 205

P.S. 206

About the Author 207

To Whom It May Concern:

You are blessed, and you are cursed. You are blessed because you have more control over your happiness than any other living creature. Yay! You are cursed for the same reason. Nay! Control sounds good in theory, but it's a lot of responsibility.

Picture a kitten. It has it easy. It does not think to itself, "What should I be when I grow up?" When it grows up, it does not ponder spiritual cat questions like, "Is it true I have nine lives?" Nor does it worry about its image, wondering, "Do the others think I'm a cool cat?" Life is simpler for cats.

You are not a cat. You are a human. What complicates things is that you are not the only human. Not only do you have to deal with your own thoughts, feelings, and behavior—the good, the bad, and the ugly. But you must also put up with other humans' thoughts, feelings, and behavior. I know, right? And then there are the circumstances, inanimate objects, and other stuff that sometimes affect your happiness.

Life feels complicated because it is. Don't let anyone tell you otherwise. But there are approaches to life that lead to happiness. One approach (let's call it Approach-A) is to pick a purpose for your life, set your own goals and work hard to achieve them, focus on the people and interests that matter most to you, be kind and generous to others along the way, figure out a way to find inner peace, and then, abracadabra; you'll be happy.

Approach-A sounds like a great way to achieve happiness, doesn't it? Well, it's not. People who follow that approach are weird. They have to think for themselves instead of following the crowd. They have to put in the effort to get the results they want. They have to do things they don't feel like doing. They have to consider other people's perspectives and not just their own. It's way too hard to follow Approach-A.

You may want to consider a different path to achieving happiness (let's call it Approach-EZ). It's way easier. It's the path most traveled by most people, most of the time. And you know most people are super happy, so obviously this approach works.

The theory behind Approach-EZ is that the simplest way to be happy is to always get your way. Failing that, you should at least be able to react to people and situations in whatever way comes naturally to you, given your personality. Under no circumstances should you have to adapt to others or to reality. Let others and reality adapt to you.

To achieve happiness via Approach-EZ, you must follow 100 simple rules. Each rule benefits you directly, indirectly, or not at all (no system is perfect). But taken collectively, the rules will lead to happiness because they take all the guesswork out of how to live your life. Bonus: Most of the rules require minimal effort.

Now, you may be tempted to stop reading before finishing the book because some rules may sound counterintuitive and/or contradict other rules. But that's by design. The rules work in mysterious ways. ChatGPT told me that most readers abandon books after the first 25% to 50%. Don't be a ChatGPT statistic. If you don't read to the end, you'll never discover the secret to a happy life. What a shame.

Also, F. Scott Fitzgerald said: "The test of a first-rate intelligence is the ability to hold two opposing ideas in mind at the same time and still retain the ability to function." If you're a brainiac who can hold two opposing ideas in your mind at the same time, consider each rule as stated (Approach-EZ) and simultaneously consider the opposite of the rule (Approach-A). Since you're a smarty-pants, you can follow the rules, flip the rules, create your own rules, or whatever. But everyone else should follow the rules.

Following are the 100 simple rules for a crappy—I mean happy—life. Give yourself 1 point for each rule you regularly follow. The goal is to score 100, but don't feel bad if you fall short. You're only human, after all.

RULE 1

Cultivate indifference to things that don't affect you

We all know there is injustice in the world, but what's it to you? Does thinking about it make you happy? No. Does it affect your lifestyle? No. Does it make you money? No. Does it give you power? No. So why should you care? It's not your fault that crime, terrorism, inequality, natural disasters, drug addiction, and homelessness exist. You didn't do it. So, when you hear about tragedies on the news, change the channel. Compassion is not entertaining. It can make you sad and cost you time and money if it prompts you to make donations. Of course, you also don't want to feel guilty, so it's best to feel nothing at all. Just ask an anesthesiologist.

RULE 2

Be impatient when you want something

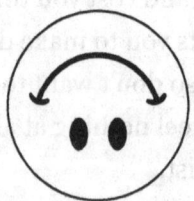

Good things come to those who wait, but they come faster to those who don't wait. And why should you have to wait on other people? As if what's going on in their lives is as important as what's going on in yours. Contrary to popular belief, patience is not a virtue. That's just an old wives' tale started by old wives. Patience is a vice. Have you ever noticed that "patience" and "patients" sound alike? That's because patients who practice patience die before the physician gets around to seeing them. Impatience is the true virtue. An impatient patient will ring their call button so frequently that the nurses will beg the physician to put them at the top of the list. And that, my friend, is why you should be impatient. It saves lives.

RULE 3

Act on your feelings of jealousy

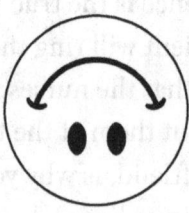

Some may call jealousy the green-eyed monster as if that's bad, but they've clearly never seen a Disney Pixar movie. Green-eyed monsters are adorable. And you should give in to feelings of jealousy even if you have brown or blue eyes. Jealousy is nature's way of saying, "Houston, we have a problem." You wouldn't feel jealous unless someone has, or is trying to take, something that's rightfully yours. Acting on your jealousy is just righting a wrong so you can get back to your happy place. So if you see your boyfriend Ken talking to his "friend" Barbie, go ahead and slash his tires and burn down her Malibu house. Her place is probably insured, and he'll think it's sweet you care enough to fight for him.

RULE 4

Practice indecisiveness

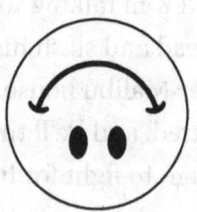

It's crucial that you not make any decisions yourself. That's what other people are for. If you're unsure what to do, ask the people around you. They've been telling you what to do your whole life anyway. You might as well listen. If you make your own decisions, you could screw up. Others may give you bad advice, but at least that gives you a scapegoat. If you absolutely must decide something all by yourself, take a long time to do it and then quickly change your mind. The quicker, the better. Constantly be second-guessing yourself. Third-guessing is even better.

RULE 5

Procrastinate for as long as you can

Procrastinate on hard things and things you don't want to do. If you wait long enough, you may not have to do anything. Issues may magically disappear, and decisions may miraculously make themselves. Of course, you can't procrastinate on everything indefinitely. Like you should probably avoid getting fired for continually missing deadlines if you have a family to support. (But no judgment here if you believe it's every man, woman, and third grader for themselves.) You may need to do some things eventually, but not until it's absolutely necessary. For instance, maybe you should eat better, move more, and stress less, but you can always do that later—like after your first heart attack. And perhaps you should be nicer to your spouse, but what's the hurry? Worst-case scenario, they'll leave you, and you'll spend the rest of your life alone. There's no need to rush things. You'll get the hang of procrastinating—it just takes time.

RULE 6

Get results without effort

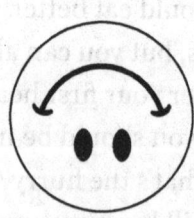

You don't need to invest time and energy to get results. Just find a good shortcut. Don't change your diet or exercise to lose weight. For $19.99, you can buy a gadget that will lose weight for you. But wait, there's more. If you act now, you can get a second gadget for the cost of shipping and handling that will also clean your house, cook your meals, and drive the kids to school. Are you looking to make a lot of money? Don't work hard. Just take a course at the introductory low price of $49.99 that will show you step-by-step how to make billions in just 10 minutes a day. I'm sure that's how Mark Zuckerberg, Jeff Bezos, and Bill Gates did it.

RULE 7

Complain as much as possible

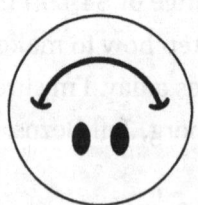

Complaining does wonders for your mood and attracts friends and admirers. People love hanging out with constant complainers. They'll want to spend more time with you, especially if they feel up and need someone to bring them down. You'll get their full sympathy because they'll realize your life is much harder than theirs. Make sure you complain about everything, including that sock you lost in the dryer last week. Tragic. A bonus to complaining is that it gives you a perfectly valid excuse for avoiding responsibility. How are you supposed to get anything done when everyone and everything is getting on your last nerve? It's annoying, and complaining is the only way to get it off your chest and onto others' chests. So carry on, Debbie Downer.

RULE 8

Criticize people to make them better

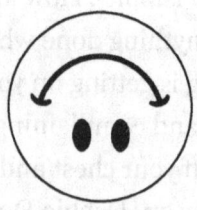

When you see a chance to point out someone's faults, do it. People may not like being criticized, but deep down, they know you're doing it for their own good. You want them to be better people, like you. No need to be mean about it unless you think it will help. Just point out all their flaws and maybe categorize and alphabetize them in PowerPoint. How will they improve if they don't know what's wrong with them? A side benefit of criticizing others is that you can feel better about yourself by comparison. It's a twofer! Also, don't limit yourself to criticizing people to their face. Be sure to also criticize them behind their back. That way, other people can also give them helpful reminders about all their faults that need fixing. We're all in this together. Let's all be our best selves. You go first.

RULE 9

Worry incessantly

One of the dumbest expressions in the world is "no worries." There are many things to worry about, and you need to consider every one of them. Especially the ones you have no control over—like what others say and do. Some fools say, "It's all good," and yada, yada, yada. Tune them out. I don't care what their T-shirts say, life is *not* good, and you *do* need to worry. If you don't, who will? You should lie awake every night thinking about everything that *is* wrong and everything that could *go* wrong. Worrying shows you care and has been proven to bring about positive changes. For best results, close your eyes, tap your heels together 3 times, and repeat, "I worry each day to keep troubles at bay" until you finally drift off to sleep at 3 a.m.

RULE 10

Start fights

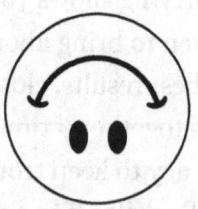

If you can't bring yourself to get into physical fights (not everyone is cut out for it), you at least need to know how to start an argument. Starting fights lets people know you're in control and won't be pushed around. It also keeps them in line. Better to be feared than liked. Try it. It's easy. If some jerk looks at you funny, challenge them to a duel. If some moron disagrees with your opinions, body slam them into a wall. Read negative meaning into everything people say and call them on it. Don't be concerned if family and friends start to avoid you. They know you're right and they're wrong, and avoiding you is just their cowardly way of admitting it. And even if you end up alone, you'll have that warm, smug feeling of knowing you were right—every time, with everybody, about everything. Fight for your right to be right.

RULE 11

Don't stand up for others

When someone is being gossiped about, you get right in there and add your two cents (or more if you can afford it). Don't feel constrained by the truth, either. If you need to tell a little black lie to impress other gossipers, you do what you have to do. Of course, they will talk about you when you're not around, but who cares? You're going to talk about them, too, so whatever. The important thing is to feed off the crowd mentality while you're still in the midst of the crowd. So, if you notice someone being bullied, jump in and help the bully. If you don't have the heart to join in the bullying, stand by and do nothing—it's the least you can do.

RULE 12

Be as selfish as you can get away with

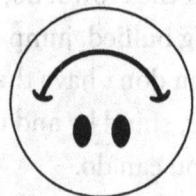

While image-conscious people try to avoid appearing selfish, they don't mind when others are selfish. In fact, they secretly envy people who are only out for number one. They wish they had the guts to pull it off. Develop a reputation for selfishness, and you'll earn the admiration of family, friends, and total strangers. Ask people to do things for you all the time—help you move, loan you money, babysit your kids—but never reciprocate. When they ask you for a favor, come up with a great excuse like, "I really wish I could, but I can't. I'm sure you understand." You don't want an armband that says WWJD? You want one that says WIIFM? If you don't know what that means, you need to work on your selfish game.

RULE 13

Don't be grateful

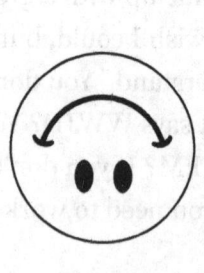

You might think it will make you feel good to be filled with gratitude, but it's a bad idea. First, if you're grateful to someone, you'll feel compelled to do something nice for them. And then they'll do something nice for you, and you'll have to do something else nice for them—it never ends. It becomes a virtuous cycle. And a burden. Second, people do nice things so they can take credit for their good deeds, so why should you show any appreciation? They should be thanking you for making them look good. Third, gratitude tends to change your outlook on life. It starts small. First, you appreciate people, and that improves your relationships. Then you appreciate your health, and that makes you take better care of yourself. Before you know it, you'll appreciate life in general. But then you'll lose your edge. I've seen it happen. So even if a Good Samaritan saves your life, don't be grateful. Sue them for ripping your favorite shirt while performing CPR on you.

RULE 14

Blame your problems on other people

It's easy to avoid personal responsibility by blaming others for your problems. Let's say you have a harmless little habit of consuming 3 or 4 bottles of wine a day. Well, before anyone can accuse you of drinking too much, go off on them and tell them they're a waste of human space. Put them on the defensive. Tell them you wouldn't have to resort to drinking if it weren't for their (fill in the blank) habit. The beauty of blaming others is that you never have to change your behavior. Only losers take responsibility for their own actions. The rest of us get to pretend all our problems are somebody else's fault. Works every time. Placing blame is the name of the game. Play irresponsibly.

RULE 15

Talk about what you're going to do, but don't do it

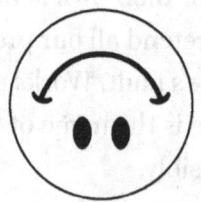

Action is highly overrated. If you never act, you can't fail. Talk about a safety net! It's much better to talk than to do. It's OK to think about things indefinitely. Do some research. Read some books. Deliberate about the pros and cons. Ask other people what they think. Just don't actually do anything. All talk and no action gives you the best of both worlds. You get to dream big (and impress people who don't know you well), but you never have to bother with that pesky implementation thing. If someone is rude enough to ask why you've never done anything you talked about, say you changed your mind and are working on something even bigger. Then talk about it ad nauseam. And if some jackass calls you all hat and no cattle, show them your cattle prod.

RULE 16

Ignore health and wellness data

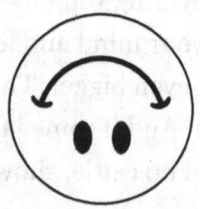

There's a different cockamamie theory about health and wellness every week. Eat this; don't eat that. Ignore all that nonsense. Keep it simple. "Eat fast food, way too much, mostly fries." As for drinking, if it's liquid, it must be hydrating. Ergo, all drinks are good for you, so don't worry about irrelevant data like sugar or alcohol content. With regard to exercise, any kind of movement is good. If you can get in and out of your recliner, you're fine. As for the sun, it doesn't cause cancer; it causes beautiful tans. And as far as stress goes, don't be a candy-ass. Suck it up. Don't bother doing so-called de-stressors like meditation—they don't work. Don't go within, go without.

RULE 17

Get upset
over petty stuff

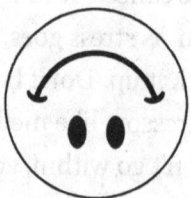

If your computer isn't working right, yell at it, bang your fist on it, and throw it out the window. That will teach it! Get so riled up that the vein on the side of your head pulses. That always helps matters. The world should never inconvenience or disappoint you. If some thoughtless person leaves their shopping cart in the middle of the grocery aisle, dump their stuff out. If your server puts a lemon in your water when you specifically requested a lime, complain loudly, don't leave a tip, and blast them on social media. Why must people intentionally ruin your day? Products should always work perfectly, and service should always be flawlessly performed. How else can you be perpetually happy? Some may claim that if everything worked perfectly, that would be Utopia, which doesn't exist. Shows how little they know. Utopia does exist. It's a small town in Uvalde County, Texas. And the servers there *never* forget the lime!

RULE 18

Ignore the Golden Rule

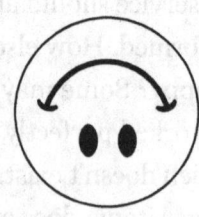

The Golden Rule is just an outdated rule about reciprocity. You do not have to *do* unto others as you would have them *do* unto you. Nor should you, especially if you're a sadomasochist who wants to flog others because you'd like them to flog you. No thanks, weirdo. A newer version of the Golden Rule (the Silver Rule?) says *do not* do unto others what you *would not* have them do unto you. That's basically about not being a hypocrite—if thou dost not want to be robbed, then thou shalt not rob others. But you don't have to follow that rule either. Others should do what you want; it makes no difference what you do... or do not do...unto them. What's wrong with a double standard? It's twice as good as a standard. Do what you want. Other people don't matter.

RULE 19

Control other people

People should think and do what you want them to. Some might say they have a right to their beliefs, but I beg to differ. Your world revolves around you, and you have a right to control what the people in your orbit think, feel, and do. If a family member doesn't agree with you on politics, money, or wearing white after Labor Day, use the silent treatment until they fall in line. If your friendly neighbor wants to move to another city for a new romance and great job, use guilt trips until they agree to stay put. How selfish of them to choose their happiness over yours. What are you supposed to do? Make new friends and mow your own lawn? Use shaming, intimidation, or harassment if you have to, but never give up control over other people. Remember what Winston Churchill said, "Never, never, never give up." Winnie was a bit melodramatic, but you get his point.

RULE 20

Let other people control you

If you're not into controlling other people, it behooves you to be the one controlled. It makes life simpler. You don't need to have a say in your own life. It's too stressful. Why bother coming up with your own interests, values, and goals when so many people out there are willing to force theirs on you? Yes, of course, they're going to do what is in their self-interest, not yours. Duh. They're controlling, not stupid. But having someone else control your life takes the pressure off you. Make sure you succumb to all the different ways people can control you. Guilt? Check. Manipulation? Check. Appeals to your vanity? Check. Appeals to your sympathy? Check. If you're not going to be the puppet master, at least be the puppet. And don't forget to smile when they pull your strings.

RULE 21

Believe everything you hear

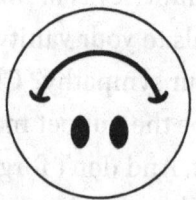

If the media, influencers, or celebrities say something, it must be true. They wouldn't say it if it weren't. The same goes for politicians, business leaders, and financial executives. You can trust them completely. They always put their constituents, clients, and customers first, and you can take that to the too-big-to-fail bank. You also want to believe and follow all the advice of authority figures, like your chain-smoking doctor, your broke financial advisor, and your recently disbarred lawyer. Suspend disbelief and trust everything the experts tell you. Fact-checking is for editors.

RULE 22

Stay in your comfy zone

Your comfy zone is nice and cozy. Why try something new that might cause you stress? Leave the experimentation to scientists. Some will argue that getting outside your comfort zone leads to personal growth, but that's fake news. You don't want to risk looking foolish. What would people think of you if you failed? All the talk about risk vs. reward is nonsense. No reward is worth the temporary anxiety of venturing into the great unknown. Stick with what's familiar. It's safer and easier. And if your heart occasionally yearns for more, ignore it. It's probably just heartburn.

RULE 23

Curb the impulse to help family and friends

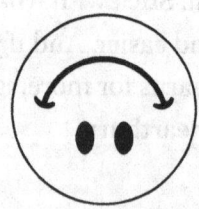

The impulse to help is just a genetic defect. Helping family and friends can only lead to bad things. They will take advantage of you. Don't be a patsy. Let other people help. That said, it doesn't hurt to take credit for helping. Whether you donated to a friend's charity or not, say you did. Nobody checks. Helping others is exhausting and costs you time and money. If you're going to help anyone, help yourself. The world helps those who help themselves. Unfortunately, we all have a heart, but yours could get you in trouble. Just resist the urge to help others when it sneaks up on you. If a family member calls asking for help, change your number.

RULE 24

Carefully cultivate your image

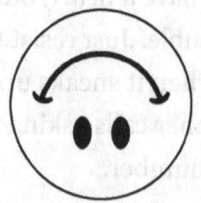

Reality is irrelevant. What matters is what other people think of you. Avoid doing something if you're not good at it so no one will know. If your life is boring, create an online image that makes you sound fascinating. If you want to look younger, cosmetically change all your features and shop in the junior department. If you're not as wealthy as your friends, max out your credit cards by buying expensive clothes, jewelry, and cars so you can keep up with them. Most importantly, remember that advertisers are your best friends when it comes to cultivating your image. They only have your best interests at heart. So if *Town & Country* says all the cool kids are buying thoroughbred horses, you need to pony up!

RULE 25

Spend your money as fast as you make it

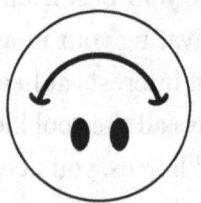

Some people say you should save your money for a rainy day, but that's only if you live in Seattle. Seriously, if you live in a sunny climate, you do not need to save for a rainy day. Just buy whatever you want because you deserve it. Anyway, you can always make more money—counterfeiters do it all the time. And don't get me started on the false rumor that saving leads to financial freedom. Financial freedom is a myth. The only people who have wealth either inherited it or stole it. So, don't bother saving. And for goodness sake, don't listen to those who say money can't buy you happiness. Of course it can. You need stuff to be happy, and you need lots of it. So, buy it...or charge it. Credit cards aren't real money anyway.

RULE 26

Don't try to figure out what's important to you

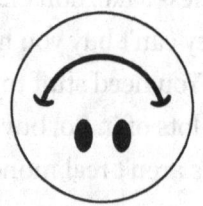

Clearly, figuring out what's important to you is wasted time. What matters to everyone else is what should matter to you. What you think doesn't count. If your culture prizes independence, be independent. If your culture prizes humility, be humble. It doesn't even have to be your culture—it could be your spouse, parents, children, friends, boss, or goldfish. Just value what others value—money, looks, power, whatever. It simplifies life. You may think knowing what's important to you will make you happier, but that's just a suburban myth. Unless you live in the city; then it's an urban legend.

RULE 27

Overthink everything

The next best thing to not thinking at all is to overthink everything. It gives your mind something to do at all times. Overanalyze this morning's conversation with your spouse. Replay past financial mistakes in your head and think through the hundreds of ways you can avoid them in the future. Obsess about worst-case scenarios at work and what you'll do if they happen. You're not going to resolve anything with all your overthinking, but that's not the point. The point is to tie yourself up in mental knots. It's a good workout. Overthinking is like a Houdini trick—you can't escape it. Throw in a few strong emotions for good measure and work yourself into a state of mental constipation. Don't stop until your migraine headache exceeds your pain threshold. If it gets too bad, ask your doctor to prescribe overthinking pills.*

*Side effects may include anxiety, sleeplessness, irritability, analysis paralysis, inability to focus, and an uncontrollable urge to become a boat captain in the Caribbean.

RULE 28

Plan everything or nothing

Either plan everything or plan nothing. You need to pick a side and stick with it—there's no middle ground here. If you're a planner, put those anal-retentive, control-freak tendencies to work and plan everything down to the last detail. That includes marking your calendar for one month before your herbs and spices expire so you can start scouting for coupons to replace them economically before their expiration date. If you're impulsive, let your spontaneous, free-spirit flag fly and plan nothing at all. So if you can make it to your own wedding, great...but don't lose any sleep over it.

RULE 29

Try to meet everyone's expectations

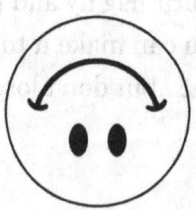

A good life is one in which you've met everyone's expectations except your own. In fact, you probably shouldn't bother having any expectations for your own life. That would imply setting a bar, but drinking in one is much easier. Anyway, by the time you're done trying to make everyone else happy by meeting their expectations, you'll be too tired to work on yours. Maybe someday, after everyone else has moved away or passed on, you can fulfill your personal expectations. On second thought, scratch that. You'll be too old to remember what they were by then.

RULE 30

Be a taker, not a giver

It's better to receive than to give. Keep score of what others do for you and what you do for others. Just kidding, it doesn't matter what you do for others. But you need to ensure that other people are continually giving you what you want. Look for people who are especially easy to take advantage of. You know, those people who are too nice for their own good but not too nice for yours. Make them feel guilty if they ever tell you no. Cry if it helps. I mean, how dare they refuse to give you their right kidney just because they gave you the left one last year? Some people are so selfish.

RULE 31

Only do what you feel like doing

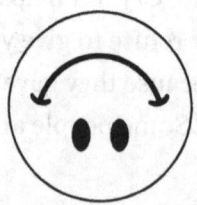

If you want to smoke, then smoke. If you want to goof off, then goof off. If you don't want to exercise, then don't exercise. Instant gratification gets a bad rap. Why are instant replay, instant messaging, and instant oatmeal OK, but people are prejudiced against instant gratification? That's discrimination. And don't worry about karma. It's not really a thing. You can ignore your health with no ill effects. You can ignore your family without hurting your relationship with them. You can avoid working and still make tons of money. Don't listen to those who say current actions affect future results. Who are they, Buddha? If it feels good, do it. If it doesn't, don't. It won't have any effect on your future.

RULE 32

Be a perfectionist

No one is capable of perfection, but that's precisely the point. You'll try to be perfect, and you'll fail. But that shouldn't keep you from seeking perfection, even if you drive yourself and everyone else crazy. You'll try harder when you're perpetually dissatisfied because you think you're capable of perfection. If that becomes too frustrating, you'll throw up your hands and toss in the towel. And who can blame you? You came, you tried, you failed. The secret to perfectionism is to let it keep you from completing anything. In fact, why even get started if success isn't guaranteed? Just stick to things you know you can do perfectly...like tying your shoelaces.

RULE 33

Hold extremist political views

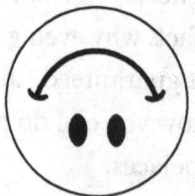

Holding moderate views is so 1990s. You want to be either far left with the jokers or far right with the clowns. Don't be stuck in the middle alone. The polarization of society has led to extreme happiness for both sides. It's incredible how it has brought family and friends together in harmony. Civility is at an all-time high. So, for crying out loud, do *not* listen to the other side, get involved in your community, or spend time with people who aren't like you. You may start to like them despite their boneheaded views. Or worse, their views might rub off on you. It's safer to stay in your echo chamber or hunkered down in your bunker.

RULE 34

Take things personally

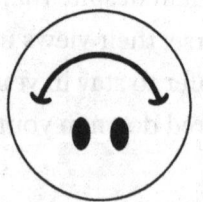

It's important that you take everything personally because everything *is* personal. If someone cuts you off in traffic, they are clearly disrespecting you. If a friend forgets your birthday, they obviously don't care about you. If your boss puts your name last on an email, they're definitely slighting you. If your spouse seems testy, they're unquestionably mad at you. People don't do things because they're in a hurry, preoccupied with other things, or just because. If it affects you, it's about you. And don't assume people are dealing with their own issues. They only do that on their own time, not when what they say or do affects you. That's "you" time. You need to interpret everything others say, do, don't say, or don't do as being about you. Because it is. If it weren't, they'd be saying, doing, not saying, and not doing it to someone else.

RULE 35

One-up people at every opportunity

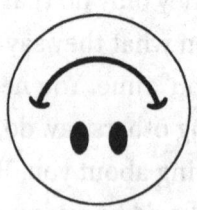

People need to know you're better than them. Let's face it: you *are* better than them. So, if someone brings up a book they're reading, be sure to say it sounds cute and then mention the Pulitzer Prize-winning novel you just finished. If they mention a popular movie they saw, bring up the foreign film you just saw (without subtitles, of course). If they mention their little trip to Iowa, mention your glamping adventure in Botswana. One-upping people is easy once you get the hang of it. You just need to top whatever they say. And if you can't top them, respond with a tight smile and a, "Well, aren't you special?" That will put them in their place while making you look morally superior. Well played.

RULE 36

Act entitled if you had a privileged upbringing

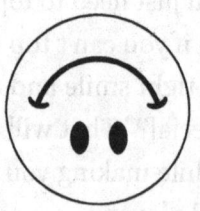

If you were born into a wealthy family and had a privileged upbringing, lord it over less fortunate people. Say things like, "Well, if I could get into an Ivy League school, it's just sheer laziness if other people can't." As if your wealthy parents' bribes had anything to do with it! Please. Poke fun at the homeless, honk at the old lady driving too slowly, and complain about the baby who had the audacity to cry on the airplane. Making the world a better place belongs on a bumper sticker, not in your heart. You do your part. You donate to the whatever-you-call-it charity every year, and it's not entirely because of the tax write-off, your name on a building, or getting to gloat to your friends about how you help the little people. What more do people want from you? Ingrates!

RULE 37

Don't be a team player

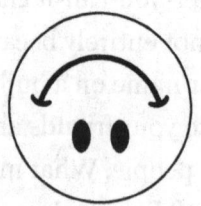

The saying, "There's no 'I' in team is stupid because there is a 'me' in team—you just have to move some letters around. Why would you want to help others achieve a common goal? Either you can do everything yourself, or they can do everything without you. Besides, teamwork involves work. Taking credit for other people's work is OK—that's just strategic borrowing. But doing the work itself is hazardous to your health. People who think we should all work together also hug trees, drive plug-in cars, and use SPF 100 sunscreen to protect themselves from global warming. Who wants to be on a team with those nutjobs? Being a team player makes sense in limited situations, like sports. But even then, the rest of the team should be your supporting cast. Be the quarterback, not the kicker.

RULE 38

Never ask for help

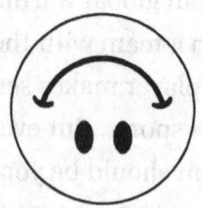

Asking for help is a sign of weakness. It shows you can't handle things on your own. You should never have to rely on anyone else for anything at any time for any reason. Be self-sufficient like the pioneers. If they could make their own clothes, grow their own crops, and build their own homes, surely you can provide for your own needs. Don't be a slacker. Only children under 10 and seniors over 100 need help from others. Everyone else should pull their own weight. "Help wanted" should be reserved for restaurant signs. And if someone asks you if you need help, say no. Then punch them in the nose. Then ask if *they* need help.

RULE 39

Don't bother
with details

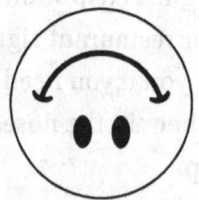

Details are irrelevant. Be the big-picture person. For instance, if you're starting a business, there's no need to do market research. What matters is that you have a fantastic idea that no one has ever thought of. Maybe you could create a phone that can do things besides make phone calls. Or perhaps you could pioneer the concept of adding a drive-up window to a restaurant that serves food really fast. And don't bother trying to understand numbers. You'll never need that information. And anyway, you can always hire other people to handle financial stuff, like that nice Madoff guy. Leave the details to the bean counters.

RULE 40

Seek the approval of others

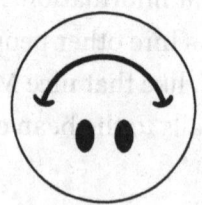

Your happiness depends on others. You can tell you're on the right track if you're referred to as a people pleaser. That's high praise! Figure out what people want from you and then give it to them. In return, they'll like you. If your family expects you to take care of everything, do it. It might exhaust you, but it will allow you to stay in their good graces. You should also seek validation in your work life. Try to collect as many pats on the back as possible. If your boss and co-workers drop the ball on a project, you be the one to catch it. Sure, it might ruin your plans for the weekend again, but there will be other weekends. And don't worry that people might take advantage of you. They'd never use your need for approval to manipulate you. And if you think you hear them calling you a sucker behind your back, it's just your imagination. They're probably talking about Halloween candy.

RULE 41

Don't seek excellence

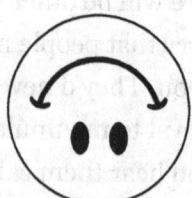

Seek to be adequate. You don't need to be outstanding. Only overachievers seek excellence. There's no shame in seeking mediocrity. Good enough is good enough. Stay in the middle of the pack and do just enough that you don't get fired but not so much that you get noticed. People don't really expect you to give it your all, nor should they. If you gave it your all, you'd have nothing left. If you're getting close to being in the zone, change lanes. And if you're in a state of flow, I sincerely hope you're in the restroom.

RULE 42

Squander your potential

Living up to your potential is just a new-age slogan. It's better to sit on your potential. It's not going to go anywhere. Your potential will still be there if you decide to use it someday. It's not like skills and talents get rusty if you don't use them. In fact, if you use them, you might wear them out. Anyway, how embarrassing if you find out you're not as good as you thought you were. The secret to happiness is never doing anything to push yourself. That way, people will always say you have potential. They'll never know what you are capable of, and neither will you. Everyone loves a mystery.

RULE 43

Stop learning after you get out of school

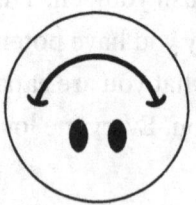

We have been brainwashed into believing lifelong learning is a good thing. It is not a good thing. It requires you to be curious, which kills cats. Everything you need to know you learned in kindergarten (or preschool if you were really advanced). The rest is just a conspiracy to convince you there is more to life than adult coloring books. There's not. Once you're done with school, learn to coast. If you do something impressive, stop. You're done. It's impolite to brag, so don't do anything else worth bragging about. If your school years were your glory days, so be it. Besides, everyone loves to hear about how you won a perfect attendance award in kindergarten. Milk it for all it's worth.

RULE 44

Never do anything bold

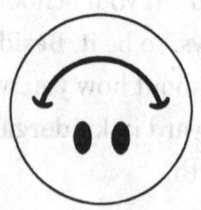

Timidity should be your goal. Risk is to be avoided at all costs. You want to aim for security and obscurity. Be meek; you're more likely to inherit the earth (just watch out for those inheritance taxes). If you do anything that's different or that raises eyebrows, you're drawing unwanted attention to yourself. Quit it. Get back in line with the rest of the gang. Boldness has no genius, power, or magic in it—Goethe was drunk when he said that.

RULE 45

Set vague goals

If you're going to set goals, at least keep them vague with no deadlines. That gives you flexibility. Setting clear goals is just setting you up for failure. For example, if you set a goal to get to a specific weight by a particular date by eliminating sugary drinks and processed foods and running for 30 minutes a day, 5 days a week... that's too much clarity. You'll clearly either achieve or fail to achieve the goal—probably the latter. Why not give yourself some wiggle room and just say you'll eat better and exercise more? If it can't be measured, no one can prove you *didn't* achieve your goal, not even you. Setting and achieving clear goals takes discipline and commitment. But you don't need those if you're not in the military. There's no need to be all you can be. Just wander aimlessly through life being some of what you can be.

RULE 46

Impress people with your intelligence

Use ostentatious words to show people you're smarter than everyone else, including them. The bigger the word, the better. If you can work "pneumonoultramicroscopic-silicovolcanoconiosis" into a conversation, you should. Mundane, single-syllable words are ubiquitous. Why bore people with pedestrian words when you can dazzle them with sesquipedalian terms? Pontificate whenever possible, and your erudite oration will make others appreciate your sagacity. Don't worry about whether people will understand you. They won't. That's fine. You want to obfuscate and confuse them. It confirms that you're a genius and makes them doubt their intelligence. That's why you're a Mensa member, and they're not. Wear your T-shirt proudly.

RULE 47

Beware of anything fun or adventurous

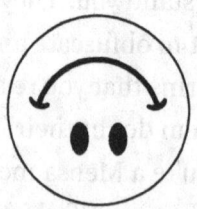

If something is fun, it's probably selfish, immoral, and a waste of time. Your time would be better spent watching grass grow and paint dry. If something is adventurous, it's probably going to kill you. The world is a terrible place. Bad things happen here. You know what happened when Columbus sailed off on his adventure in 1492, right? He discovered the world was flat, and he fell off the ocean to his death. Consider yourself warned.

RULE 48

Hang out with negative people

You can count on negative folks to tell it like it is. They can point out everything wrong with your opinions and plans. They can help you justify inaction and avoid disasters. Being around them drains your energy and brings you down, so you'll be too tired and depressed to do anything anyway. If being around them gives you a headache, pop an aspirin. Their helpful advice ensures your life will never, ever change. Better still, you'll get to keep hanging out with them—for the rest of your life. Whatever you do, *do not* hang out with positive people. I'm not saying they're bad people. I'm sure they mean well. But if you start listening to them, they'll fill your head with pipe dreams of how great your life could be. As if! Just stay away from Pollyannas...Annas are much better company.

RULE 49

Let others compensate for your disorganization

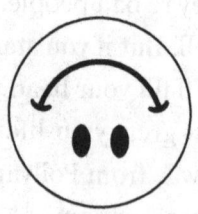

Getting organized may improve your productivity and relationships, but it's a hassle. Who has time for it? Certainly not you—you're too busy to be bothered by such a plebeian task. You're not a secretary, or administrative assistant, or whatever they're calling themselves these days. Never mind that you inconvenience other people. So what if they have to cover for you constantly? And prompt you to do what you said you were going to do. And remind you when and where you're supposed to show up and what you're supposed to bring. Uh, that's their problem, not yours. It's too much effort to take two whole minutes to put something on your calendar. Just count on other people to pick up the slack for your disorganization. Why else would you keep them around?

RULE 50

Don't look for humor in life

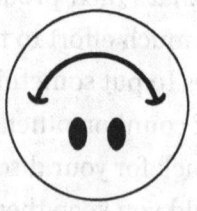

Life is deadly serious, and you should be, too. You shouldn't try to see the humor in life because there isn't any. How can you make jokes when the Javan rhino is threatened with extinction? Don't you care? And it would be prudent to learn to be more politically correct. You should never say anything that could potentially cause any offense to anybody at any time in any place for any reason just because you think it's funny. Why would you laugh at that bald guy who slipped and fell on a banana peel? Maybe that follically challenged man is slightly uncoordinated and didn't see the banana peel because he's visually impaired. Did you ever think of that? Because she/her/hers doesn't think it's funny at all.

RULE 51

Don't worry about the consequences of your actions

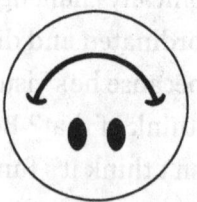

There aren't any consequences to your actions. If no one wants to be around you, it's because they're jealous of you, not because you're mean to people. If you're pleasantly plump, it's because of a thyroid problem, not because you eat crappy food and don't exercise. If you're pencil-thin, it's because of high metabolism, not because you eat like a bird. If you've been fired from ten jobs in a row, it's because your bosses were racist, sexist pigs, not because you called in sick every day. There are *no* consequences to your actions. Never have been, never will be. So be as irresponsible as you want. The only thing that will come back to bite you is a pissed-off snake.

RULE 52

Never change, and don't believe others who claim to have changed

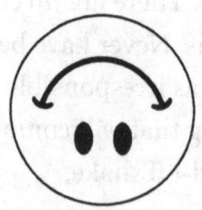

Human nature doesn't change, and you're a human. Do the math. Keep thinking the same thoughts, doing the same things, going to the same places, and hanging out with the same people for the rest of your life. Stagnation is good. Change takes work, which is a four-letter word. And change takes time, which is also a four-letter word. So why do it? And don't believe other people who pretend they've changed. They haven't. If someone was a jerk in middle school, they're still a jerk today. They may fool other people—their spouse, children, friends, and the idiot who awarded them the Medal of Honor—but you know better. So continue to treat them like the 12-year-old who gave you a wedgie. And if you ever get the chance, return the favor.

RULE 53

Monopolize conversations

Other people want to know everything about you—what you're thinking, what you've been doing, where you got your new shoes. They can't get enough of hearing about you, so give the people what they want. And don't feel you need to ask about them. Assume everything is on a need-to-know basis, and you don't need to know anything about them. Compared to you, they're boring. Hearing about you is probably the highlight of their day. Hold them captive with your captivating conversation. Don't even pause for breath. If they interrupt you, interrupt their interruption. And if they excuse themselves to go to the restroom, follow them into the stall.

RULE 54

Skip the positive self-talk because words don't matter

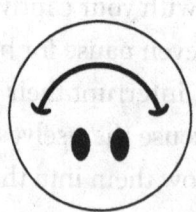

All those books about affirmations, mantras, and positive self-talk are nonsense. Telling yourself that you're healthy, wealthy, and wise doesn't cure your back pain, increase your bank account, or make you King Solomon. They're just words, and everyone knows that words don't matter. Seriously, test it for yourself. Next time a cop pulls you over for speeding, tell him to get the f*ck out of your face, and you'll see your words have no impact whatsoever. He'll probably even let you off with a warning.

RULE 55

Express your anger when things don't go your way

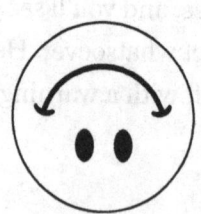

It's perfectly fine to explode when people make you angry. It keeps them on their toes. The ability to get people to walk on eggshells is a highly coveted skill. It ensures you'll usually get your way. Be creative in how you express your anger, too. Don't just yell, pound your first, or withdraw affection. If someone makes you mad, get them fired, spread lies about them, file a false police report, throw their clothes out the window, and put laxatives in their food. Get angry at situations you don't like, too. Stuck in traffic? Blare on the horn and ram the car in front of you. Flight canceled? Yell at the ticket agent and throw your bag at the pilot. Venting your anger is cathartic. Don't worry about the impact on others. People are resilient. They'll be fine.

RULE 56

Never sit still

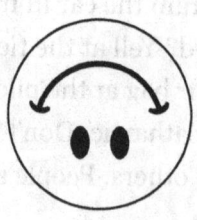

You'll have plenty of time to sit still when you're old or in a straitjacket. Until then, you should be rushing through every minute of every day of every year. Nothing's better for your health than nonstop busyness. It keeps your heart rate up, so it counts as exercise. And don't listen to people who say you need eight hours of sleep per night. Nighttime can be your most productive time because there's no one awake to bother you while you work or play video games. Downtime is for deadbeats. Try to multitask whenever possible. Just because you're giving birth doesn't mean you can't also respond to emails. They have wi-fi in hospitals.

RULE 57

Be judgmental

You should judge others based on your beliefs, opinions, and standards. In *Hamlet*, Shakespeare said, "There is nothing either good or bad, but thinking makes it so." So obviously, your thoughts on what is good or bad make it so. If you deem someone's words and behaviors to be good (i.e., in alignment with yours), you should rule in their favor. Let them know you approve and hold them out as an example to others. However, if you judge what someone says or does as bad, you must rule against them. If they insist on a hearing, tell them you already heard them. That's why you found them guilty of being wrong. Skip the innocent-until-proven-guilty part and go straight to sentencing. The punishment should fit the crime. If they're just a little misguided, let them off with a slap on the wrist. But if you judge their views or actions to be really bad, you should throw the book at them. And if it doesn't cause a concussion, you didn't throw it hard enough.

RULE 58

Never apologize

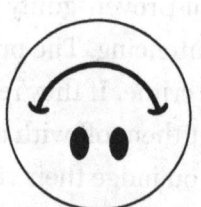

Apologizing is an admission that you did something wrong. Even if you suspect you were potentially less correct than usual, why dwell on it? There's no sense crying over spilled milk (or whatever you spilled or did). It's over. Move on. No good can come from apologizing. For one thing, it gives the other person something to hold over your head. You'll never hear the end of it. For another thing, it sets a precedent. Once you start apologizing for one thing, you'll be expected to apologize for every little thing—like forgetting to pick up the kids or gambling away your inheritance. It will never stop. When you allegedly screw up, keep a low profile for a day or two and then act like nothing happened. If the so-called wronged party brings it up again, gaslight them.

RULE 59

Keep doing what's not (yet) working

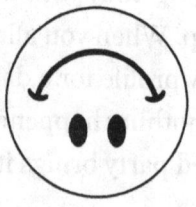

Mindless repetition is good for the soul. Just because something isn't working now doesn't mean it won't eventually work. Hang in there. There's no need to change your tactics. If you've unsuccessfully tried to quit smoking cold turkey 202 times in a row, try again. The 203rd time's a charm. If you've tried reasoning with an unreasonable relative for over 15 years, keep repeating the same old arguments. Your words are probably just taking a little time to sink in. If you repeatedly bend over backward for a friend who never reciprocates, bend over further. I'm sure they'll repay you for all you've done any day now. Practice makes perfect, so keep doing exactly what you're doing. You know what they say, "Sanity is doing the same thing over and over and expecting different results." Stay sane out there.

RULE 60

Make excuses every chance you get

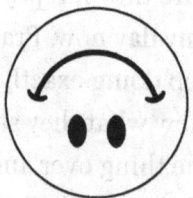

Have excuses ready for when people accuse you of anything, like: It wasn't me. It's not my fault. He started it. I was drunk. It works every time! Also, keep some excuses in your back pocket to justify inaction: I'm too young (or old). I don't have a college degree. I don't have the money. I don't have the time. My dog ate my homework. Excuses may not benefit you in the long run, but they help you save face in the short run. Making excuses is far easier than working to get what you want. Besides, maybe you'll get lucky, and things will just fall into your lap. Fingers crossed.

RULE 61

Don't commit to anyone or anything

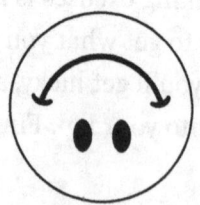

Commitment is too limiting. It narrows your options. Commitment closes too many doors that you might want to occasionally open. What if you commit to one person but then meet someone hotter? Or what if you commit to plans with a friend, but then something better comes along? Or what if you commit to school or a job, but then it interferes with your partying and sleeping in? It's just better to take a "wait and see" attitude toward life. No need to go whole hog on anything; just nibble on a few strips of bacon. You can sample different things and people; just don't stick with any of them long enough to matter. You can like them, but you don't have to put a ring on them.

RULE 62

Be fearful

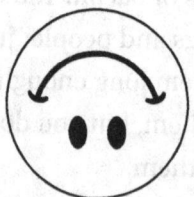

I cannot overstate the importance of fear. You absolutely must be afraid of everything, and yes, that includes your own shadow. Shadows are the devil. Think about all the terrible things in the world. Don't do anything about them but think about them. In fact, obsess over them. Sure, you could go for a walk, but what if you get mugged or a dog bites you? You could fly on an airplane, but what if it crashes? You could go to a cocktail party, but what if no one talks to you? You would die of embarrassment, and everyone would laugh at your funeral and say what a loser you were. The only thing you should *never* fear are things you might be able to do something about. For instance, don't fear dying from heart disease, cancer, or a stroke. And don't bother trying to prevent those diseases. I'm sure you're more likely to be eaten by a mountain lion.

RULE 63

Be skeptical

It's important not to trust anyone or anything. You risk being let down. It's safer to assume the worst. Then you won't be disappointed. It's especially important to doubt yourself. If you start believing in yourself, the next thing you know, good things will happen for you. But then, someday, something terrible will happen. You'll find out that someone else got your promotion, or the person you like will hook up with your best friend, or your favorite restaurant will no longer serve anchovies on pizzas, and then where will you be? Disillusioned is where. Don't risk getting your hopes up. Eventually, something will go wrong, and you'll be miserable. When in doubt, go ahead and freak out.

RULE 64

Dwell on the past

Dwelling on the past is especially important if your childhood was difficult in any way. It's pure gold. How can you be expected to succeed in life if your parents didn't raise you right? Studies show that 99.999 percent of adults had blissful childhoods, so it's unfair that your parents weren't perfect like everyone else's. You're ruined for life. There's no way you can ever move on, nor should you. If you get to a point where an unpleasant childhood memory starts to fade, dredge it back up and throw yourself a pity party. A tough childhood gives you a built-in excuse for everything for the rest of your life. But if your childhood was blissful, all hope is not lost. Have you ever had a romantic relationship turn out poorly? Well then, dwell on the heartbreak forever and take that baggage with you into all your future relationships. The future is scary. Stay stuck in the past, where at least you know how the story ends. Nobody likes surprise endings.

RULE 65

Only see things from your perspective

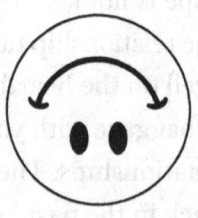

Don't even entertain the possibility that there's more than one reasonable point of view. There's not. Those who claim you might learn something and improve your relationships by considering different perspectives have smoked too much weed. Insist that your viewpoint is correct in every situation. Even if you suspect you're occasionally mistaken, and that this might be one of those times, don't let that stop you from insisting you're right. You probably are. And to make sure everyone knows it, show your disdain for anyone who disagrees with your perspective. Look down on them—literally, if you're taller. Putting your glasses on the end of your nose and peering over the top of them is also very effective. Eye rolls work, too.

RULE 66

Never forgive people

If someone in your life screws up—even if they admit it and say they're sorry—you need to keep reminding them of it daily or at least weekly. Never let them forget it. They did what they did to you 20 years ago, but it feels like it was yesterday. It still hurts. It was wrong. They need to feel bad about it forever. It's especially good to bring it up if you recently screwed up. Cut them off at the pass as soon as they bring up what you did. Remind them that at least you didn't do the horrible thing they did...that ought to shut them up. Hold grudges until the day you die. And then come back and haunt them in the afterlife.

RULE 67

Beat yourself up when you make a mistake

Fair is fair. You shouldn't forgive others when they make mistakes, so why should you forgive yourself? When you do something stupid or wrong, remind yourself of it constantly. You may even want to ask your friends to keep bringing it up lest you forget. Then you'll feel guilty, which will keep you humble, which is a good thing. You should never think about moving on or letting things go. Self-flagellation is good for the soul. You should punish yourself for eternity even if your mistake wasn't a mortal sin. Zeus punished Sisyphus by forcing him to repeatedly roll a boulder up a hill. Surely, the least you can do is walk around with a pebble in your shoe as your penance.

RULE 68

Be a doormat

Being a doormat is an excellent option if you have a timid personality. There's nothing wrong with letting people walk all over you. It makes them respect you more. You may think they're being unkind when they put you down, but maybe they're just being honest, and you really are odd and funny-looking. If you don't let what people say bother you, their words have no power over you. So, you must give them that power. And if they order you around, it's just because they trust you to do as you're told, like a good girl, boy, dog, or whatever. So if someone walks all over you, don't complain. Just take it lying down.

RULE 69

If you grudgingly agree to do something, make sure everyone knows you resent it

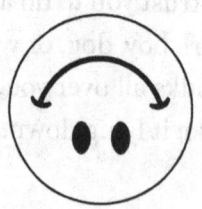

Everyone loves a martyr, so you owe it to them not to disappoint. You wanted to see that movie where that guy does that thing that he's done in every one of his prior 100 films, but the rest of your family wants to see the new movie that won 50 Oscars. Sigh and complain loudly that the movie sucks, the actors suck, and the popcorn sucks. They need to know you're suffering and that it's all their fault. Some might suck it up for their family's sake, but they have an ulterior motive. They probably love their families or some such thing. Sentimental fools.

RULE 70

Avoid persistence

Persistence takes too long. Successful people go on and on about never quitting, but they're just drama queens. If at first you don't succeed, quit. Why put in more effort if you don't get immediate results? And even if you're making *some* progress, keeping at it when you run into obstacles is no fun. If it were meant to be, it'd be easy. Resist the urge to persist. Eventually, it will disappear, and you'll free up time for more enjoyable things like eating Doritos and binge-watching your favorite show. And as for people who tell you to "keep your nose to the grindstone," they're imbeciles. Grindstones are abrasive and will make your nose bleed.

RULE 71

Don't stoop to doing menial tasks

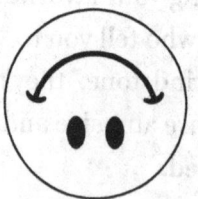

Why on earth would anyone expect you to help with menial tasks? Don't they know it's beneath you? That's for minimum-wage workers who enjoy that kind of thing. When people ask you to "pitch in," make sure they realize who they're talking to. Hand them your 10-page curriculum vitae. And if they still don't take the hint, give them your gold, embossed business card with your family crest and title: *The Most Important Person in This City, This Country, This Planet, This Century*. People can be so clueless.

RULE 72

If you're wealthy and greedy, use your money and power strictly for your benefit

If you can afford it, pay high-priced tax lawyers, wealth managers, and family offices (if you're really loaded) to shield your wealth from taxes. So what if it forces middle-income taxpayers to make up the difference? Someone has to pay for defense, infrastructure, first responders, social security, health insurance, and whatever else taxes pay for. It's not your fault they can't afford advisors to help them with tax avoidance (or tax evasion if that's how you roll). And if you're a business tycoon, make political contributions, hire lobbyists, and pay bribes to shape the laws to benefit you. While you're at it, use your corporate power to suppress employee wages and lower benefits. Oh, and screw over your vendors, too. It's just good business. And if our democracy becomes a plutocracy, so what? Didn't the Gettysburg Address call for government of the wealthy people, by the wealthy people, for the wealthy people?

RULE 73

If you're able-bodied but lazy, find ways to game the system

If working isn't really your kind of thing, feel free to take government benefits intended for children, the elderly, the disabled, and other beneficiaries. It's not like anyone will miss the pittance you're taking from Medicare, Medicaid, unemployment benefits, or whatever. I'm sure no one else is doing it, so it's not like it will impact the intended beneficiaries or taxpayers. It sounds bad when holier-than-thou types call it fraud, but what's wrong with submitting a few false claims or creating a couple of fake identities to get freebie benefits? Technically, it may be illegal, but it's not like you're a hardened criminal who jaywalks, loiters, or engages in disorderly conduct.

RULE 74

Don't be authentic

Everyone loves phony people. They're so entertaining. It's what you say, not what you really think, that counts. It's especially advisable to say and do the opposite of what you feel. Rave about the celebrity book you hated and suck up to the boss you detest. Tell people what you think they want to hear. Or what gets you what you want. Hide your genuine self and act like you value what everyone else values. If you get a funny feeling in your gut when pretending to be someone you're not, ignore it. I'm sure it's just gas. The best part is that the more time you spend being fake, the sooner you'll forget who you really are. That's helpful because then you'll no longer have to *pretend* to be somebody else; you'll actually *be* somebody else. May your true self rest in peace.

RULE 75

Be 100% consistent in your opinions

People like people who are consistent from day to day and decade to decade. Never change your opinion. If you change your beliefs willy-nilly, how can anyone trust you? Be on the lookout for others who contradict themselves, too. It's fun to catch someone doing it. Wait, what? Did you say you believe in equal pay for equal work for women? Ha—gotcha! When you were 15, you were quoted in the school paper as saying a woman's place is in the home, and she shouldn't be paid at all. Busted. Don't give me that, "But I'm 95 years old, and my views have changed." That's B.S. You know what you said—stand by it, or you're a liar and a flip-flopper. People should never change their opinion once they get around to having one.

RULE 76

Expect everything to be easy

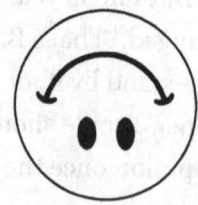

Life was not meant to be hard. Well, I mean, except at the very beginning with the whole childbirth thing. But after that, it's supposed to be smooth sailing. Everything should come easily to you. If it doesn't, you have the right to get upset and throw a tantrum. Life should conform to your wishes. You should be able to attract what you want and repel what you don't want. In your personal life, you shouldn't have to work on relationships. Other people should go along with you on everything. If they don't, get new friends and family. And in your work life...well, first, "work" life is a misnomer. It should be more like your "pay-me-to-show-up" life and not require any actual work. Work is for bees.

RULE 77

Embrace boredom

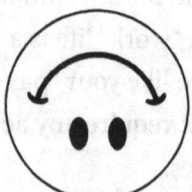

You're on the right track if you are bored and tired with yourself and your life. Curiosity, observation, imagination, and creativity are for artsy-fartsy people. Thrill seekers get all the attention, but anti-thrill seekers are happier. They are calmer, more predictable, and have lots of fabulous routines—like washing dishes at the same time every day and wearing different colored socks for each day of the week. Boredom is good because it means you're not doing anything risky, challenging, or life-altering. You want to stay in the sweet spot between "bored to tears" and "bored to death." Your goal should be a life so dull that if you wrote a memoir, no one would read it.

RULE 78

Avoid stating an opinion if possible

When someone asks what you think, turn the tables and ask what they think. People can be tricky. They act like they want your opinion, but what if it differs from theirs? Awkward. It's better to play it safe and go with the crowd. Don't just avoid sharing opinions on significant issues like politics and religion. Small opinions can lead to big ones, so it's best to avoid those, too. If you're dining out with friends, don't say what you want to eat. Just say you'll have what they're having. Whenever you're forced to give an opinion, be as wishy-washy about it as possible. For instance, it helps to say, "Well, on the one hand..." and then mention the other hand. You might even want to throw in both feet if it keeps you from being pinned down.

RULE 79

Spend all your time on your devices

It's critically important that you respond immediately every time your smartphone, tablet, computer, smartwatch, or newest thingamajig chimes, beeps, rings, vibrates, or flashes to let you know that something, somewhere, is going on. It doesn't matter if it's a call, text, email, update, or alert; you must treat it like DEFCON 1. If your device makes a sound, you need to pounce on it like a cat on catnip. Otherwise, you might miss something. Doesn't matter what you're doing or who you're with; they are not as important as your master device. If you miss your baby's first steps, you can always catch her second or third steps. It's not like you've never seen anyone walk before. What's on your device or social media feed is more important than everything else. Know what I mean, Clickbait?

RULE 80

Be oblivious

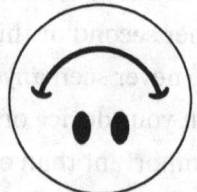

It's not necessary to pay attention to what's going on around you. The only thing that matters is what's going on in your head. Try to ignore everything else. Awareness could lead to observations and insights, which could lead to inconvenient truths. Don't let anything get in the way of the automatic thoughts that run through your head all day, every day. Becoming more aware may cause you to see reality as it is rather than how you want it to be. That means you'll see your life as it really is, which may, in turn, encourage you to make changes. Heaven forbid. It's far better to wander through life without wondering about life. Who cares? What's for dinner?

RULE 81

Never do for yourself what you can get others to do for you

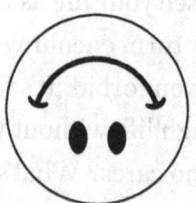

If you get others to do things for you that you could do for yourself, some may say you're lazy. That's a compliment. It shows how clever you are to get out of doing work. Why do something yourself if you can pawn it off on other people? They're there to serve you. The trick is to appeal to people's kindness and desire to be helpful. So, play the helpless card. Act overwhelmed or incompetent or feign sickness—whatever you need to do to get people to do your bidding. Try to have multiple people in your lineup, so if one says no, you have somewhere else to go. And don't worry about being a burden to others. They don't mind. Also, don't feel insulted if someone calls you a parasite—it's a term of endearment. Parasites are cute.

RULE 82

Do everything yourself

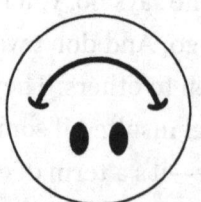

You may think this rule contradicts the prior rule about getting others to do things for you. It does. Good catch. But if you were paying attention when I described Approach-EZ, you'll remember I said it allows you to react in ways that come naturally to you *given your personality*. If you're a control freak like me, you may not want to delegate because other people will probably just screw it up. No one else can do things as well as you, so handle everything yourself. If you get burnt out, grab a fire extinguisher and get back to work. You may not be able to get as much done by not delegating, but at least everything will be done right. And you'll sleep better at night knowing that, once again, you saved the day. Excellent work, Wonder Woman.

RULE 83

Insist that everything be fair

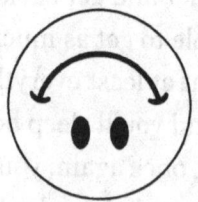

Life is supposed to be fair, and fairness is defined as biased in your favor. No one else should get an advantage you don't. Didn't get that promotion? Not fair. You work harder, and the man who got it is a brown-noser. Another poker player got lucky on the river? Not fair. You played the hand better, and he's a poker bully. Someone got the parking spot you wanted? Not fair. You were there first, and the woman who took your spot is a selfish...female dog. It doesn't matter what it is—lucky breaks, winning stakes, bigger house, better spouse—it's unfair when someone else gets what you deserve. On the other hand, if you luck out and get what someone else deserves, that's different. That's just the way the cookie crumbles. Got milk?

RULE 84

Listen to the haters

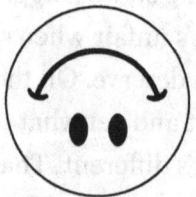

Haters are constantly putting other people down. They like to make fun of anyone whose looks, sex, race, religion, age, nationality, opinions, or zodiac signs differ from theirs. Haters like to stir up crap and divide people. It's kind of like a magic trick. They divert your attention away from their shortcomings and ulterior motives by getting you to focus instead on the person or group they're villainizing. It's pretty clever, really. And a bonus is that as long as the haters are focused on someone else, they'll leave you alone. Even better, you get a free pass to blame everything on the scapegoats, too. But be sure to carry your pass with you at all times in case you're stopped at a checkpoint.

RULE 85

Be an insensitive-sensitive person

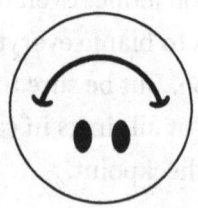

You want to be the person who can dish it out but can't take it. What idiot would want to take it? Feel free to criticize others whenever you feel like it, but don't let them pull that crap on you. Turnabout is foul play. It's OK to tell your insecure friend they have a great personality and, luckily for them, some people don't care about looks. But if someone so much as offers you a glass of low-fat milk, you should break down in tears and say you can't believe they're calling you fat. How could they be so cruel and insensitive? You would never say anything like that to them. Wink. Wink.

RULE 86

Credit your success to skill and your failures to bad luck, but credit other people's success to good luck and their failures to their weaknesses

You've earned your success the old-fashioned way through hard work and talent, but some people just get lucky. There is no way that nerdy kid from fourth grade who was always on his computer succeeded on merit. His family probably had connections in the tech world. Nepotism is so unfair. What's also unfair is when you fail due to bad luck and unforeseen circumstances. When you issued all those NINJA loans, how could you possibly have known that lending money to people with no income, no jobs, and no assets was not a sustainable practice? Certainly wasn't your fault borrowers defaulted on your good-faith loans!

RULE 87

Let a lack of knowledge hold you back

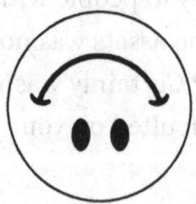

If you don't already know something, there's not much you can do about it. It's tough to find information, especially online. You need a device, an internet connection, and a browser (all rare things). Searching for answers is complicated and expensive. And artificial intelligence is making it even harder to figure things out. You have to know how to ask questions and everything. It's too much trouble. Stick with the "don't seek, don't find" policy. If the facts want you to know them, they'll appear on a TikTok video. Ignorance is bliss. Bliss out.

RULE 88

Don't reflect on your life

You may sometimes have a fleeting thought that there is more to life than how you're living it. Perish the thought. Seriously, kill it before it takes root. Get busy doing trivial things so you don't have time to think about it. Alcohol and other drugs help, too. You don't need to reflect on your thoughts, feelings, behaviors, motivations, or desires. They are what they are—end of story. If you start trying to understand yourself, then you'll start identifying your values, then you'll start evaluating your relationships, and then you might want to start making changes. It never stops. Don't think and thrive. Leave self-reflection to the monks.

RULE 89

Speak before you think

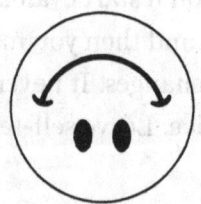

Many people think you should think before you speak to avoid saying the wrong thing. But that's just for slow people. If you're smart, you don't have to worry about it. The right words roll off your tongue automatically. If there are any misunderstandings, it's your listeners' fault, not yours. You can't help it if they heard what you said and not what you meant. Thinking before you speak takes precious time and gives others a chance to talk first. Even if you have to throw in a few "ums," "uhs," and "you knows" to stall for time, just say something to get the ball rolling and then fire away. Speak first; think later. Better yet, why think at all?

RULE 90

Don't believe
in yourself

People who believe in themselves are selfish. They have faith in themselves regardless of what other people think. They don't wait for permission to do what they want, which is rude. It's unfair to everyone else if you start turning your dreams into reality. Your effort may pay off for you, but where does that leave the rest of us? Are you trying to make us feel bad because we don't believe we can make our dreams come true? For shame. Stop believing in yourself because it shines a spotlight on everyone else. Sure, your little success story may inspire total strangers, but those who know you will either resent it or suddenly become your best friend and ride your coattails. Stop showing off and live a life of quiet desperation like everybody else. And if you must believe in someone, believe in Santa Claus.

RULE 91

Maximize your wealth and flaunt it

Money and all it can buy is the true source of happiness. Nothing else even comes close. Don't listen to people who say experiences, relationships, faith, and other immaterial things are more important; they're not. The only people who believe that are poor. Never pass up an opportunity to increase your wealth, and don't let legality or ethicality stand in your way. That's why you retain lawyers and PR firms. If you weren't fortunate enough to be born into wealth, you can always marry into it. Cash is king; that's how he got the queen. Do whatever it takes to amass wealth, and then display it prominently. Make sure the cars you drive, the homes you own, and the art you collect are worthy of envy. And always fly first class. Just joking with you—as if you would fly with the unwashed masses instead of on a private jet with your own kind!

RULE 92

Choose your friends based on their looks, money, achievements, and connections

It doesn't matter whether you like your friends or enjoy being around them. And it certainly doesn't matter whether they'll be there for you through life's ups and downs. It's not like you'd stick around for them through the downs. What's important is whether they're someone worth knowing. The litmus test is whether your other friends and acquaintances are impressed that you know them. If not, lose the deadwood. Friendships should be transactional. Unless you get more out of the friendship than what you put into it, why bother? Now, I grant you that these shallow friendships aren't likely to last very long, but who cares? Thank you, next.

RULE 93

Turn everything into a problem

It's best to always be on the lookout for problems so they don't sneak up on you. For instance, if someone buys you a gift, don't start feeling appreciative until you think it through. Do you love the gift? Did they spend enough money on you? Do you now feel pressured to buy them a gift? If your answers aren't yes, yes, and no, you have a problem. So toss the gift aside, and don't bother saying thanks. Then maybe they'll stop buying you stupid gifts. Problem solved. Problems are everywhere if you know where to look. If you don't see the problem in a situation, you're not looking hard enough. And when problems inevitably arise, don't look for a silver lining. Even if you find one, it will probably be tarnished or cheap nickel.

RULE 94

Avoid confrontation

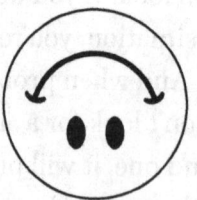

Confrontation is fine if you're willing to upset people. Otherwise, it would be best if you avoided it. Confronting someone might be more honest and empowering and bring increased respect and better relationships, but it's not worth the downsides. First, you could lose. If you confront someone, you might have to back down if they cry, yell, or hit you. Second, you may become less popular. If you stop letting a bully push you around, they may start to avoid you. That's one less person in your social group. Third, confrontation causes acute stress. Better to deal with the chronic stress of not standing up for what you believe than the temporary stress that comes from confrontations. If you must confront someone, do it quickly, apologize afterward, and run home with your tail between your legs.

RULE 95

Put limitations on yourself

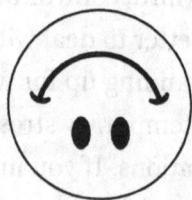

Restrictions are good. They keep you from getting too big for your britches. And who wants to have to size up? There are good reasons for limiting what you can be, do, and have. If you're too young, you don't have the necessary experience. If you're too old, no one will want to hire you. If you're too busy, you don't have time to take on new projects. If you're not a risk-taker, you can't be an entrepreneur. If you're not creative, you can't be a writer or artist. If you're not good at limiting yourself, let others do it for you. Believe them when they say you're not good enough to pursue whatever foolish idea pops into your head. It's for your own good. To preserve your ego and protect you from failure, you need to place limitations on yourself. This rule is especially important if you're older, younger, or middle-aged.

RULE 96

Play the victim

Playing the victim is pure gold. People feel sorry for you, so you can manipulate them, avoid responsibility, and get lots of attention. Even if they suspect you may be exaggerating, they won't want to appear callous, so they'll play along. Dredging up past tragedies is one way to play the victim continually. And If you can't think of a legitimate reason for your victimhood, make one up. If you have the stomach for it, you can even victimize yourself. Stand naked in the freezing rain so you'll get sick, fall down a short flight of stairs so you'll get hurt, start a fight so you'll provoke a breakup, or blow your paycheck so you can't pay your bills. That's the quadfecta: illness, accident, relationship issues, and money problems. Guaranteed to garner sympathy. And when you tell people what's going on, moan and groan so they'll pity you even more. Victimhood is the perfect crime—you can get away with murder, but nobody has to die.

RULE 97

Constantly compare yourself to others

How will you know if you're getting an A+ in life if you're not comparing yourself to others? You need to track how you're doing across all core subjects: Appearance, Career, Money, Relationship Status, Knowledge & Education, Social Status, Health & Fitness, Friends, Family Life, and Talents. Plus, consider your electives, like Travel Experiences, Books Read, Social Media Followers, your Jeep Ducks collection, etc. Life grades on a curve, so you can't just focus on how you're doing; you have to see how your grades compare to everyone else. A = Amazing. B = Brilliant. C = Common. D = Dreadful. F = Forget Grades and Turn On, Tune In, and Drop Out.

RULE 98

Jump to conclusions

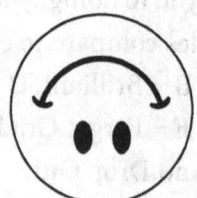

While some may encourage you to collect all the facts before reaching any conclusions, my research suggests that takes too long. There's no downside to jumping to conclusions. In fact, 5 out of 5 skydivers recommend jumping. And they're the experts. Even as a layperson, you're qualified to jump to conclusions. Go with the first thing that pops into your head. If it's right, you'll have saved a lot of time not having to ask questions or do research and analysis. And even if your conclusion is wrong, just jump to the next one.

RULE 99

Expect other people
to make you happy

Making you happy is other people's job. It's completely irrational to expect you to make yourself happy. There's only one of you, but there are tons of other people out there who can make you happy if they all work together. It's such a small thing to ask that they prioritize your happiness over theirs. Granted, you may not spend much time thinking about how to make them happy, but that's neither here nor there. Now, you may occasionally encounter someone who derives happiness from within and spreads it around. Please stay away from them; they may be contagious. You have the right to Life, Liberty, and the Pursuit of Happiness, and your happiness depends on others. It says so right there in the Declaration of Dependence.

RULE 100

Constantly chase after happiness

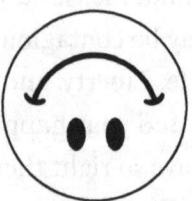

How will you achieve lasting happiness if you don't keep chasing after it? Take a cue from dogs. They catch cars because they keep chasing after them. Chasing happiness keeps you focused on what you don't have. And getting all the things you don't have is the only way to be happy. Hence, the chasing. It will take time, so you'll need to focus exclusively on yourself until you achieve a state of permanent joy. From sunup to sundown, you should think about why you're unhappy and what it will take to fix it. Don't waste time trying to change your mindset or behavior. You need other people and circumstances to change to make you happy. So keep waiting on the world to change, and someday, the stars will align, your ship will come in, you'll find your pot of gold, your knight in shining armor will appear, fortune will smile upon you, and you'll live happily ever after. THE END. P.S. Since you won't be needing it anymore, can I have your lucky rabbit's foot?

So there you have it. If you follow the 100 rules from Approach-EZ, you're guaranteed to be happy. It's not a money-back guarantee, but I'm pretty sure you'll be happy. Probably.

How'd you do?

If you scored **81-100**, you nailed it.
You're a happiness guru.

If you scored **61-80**, you stapled it.
You're a happiness expert.

If you scored **41-60**, you glued it.
You're a happiness professional.

If you scored **21-40**, you taped it.
You're a happiness beginner.

If you scored **0-20**, you paper-clipped it.
You're a happiness wannabe. (And you ain't gonna be.)

I hope you've found my crappy advice helpful. If you didn't, write your own damn book. ☺

**Lukewarm regards,
Your Friend in Happiness**

P.S.

If you're a contrarian, feel free to do the opposite of what the rules state. I'm not sure it's a good idea to be a rule breaker, but you do you. Maybe you'll get lucky and achieve fulfillment, freedom & happiness.

If you're a minimalist, feel free to ignore the happiness rules altogether. You were probably going to anyway. My advice? Focus on what's important to you and minimize whatever distracts you from it. Priceless.

For everyone else, there's Mastercard. Use yours to buy as many copies of this book as possible and share them with your friends and family so they, too, can live happily ever after.

About the Author

Kara Lane has published multiple books on multiple subjects. She's been advised to pick a niche and stick to it (it helps build a readership), but she doesn't listen well. She tends to write about whatever interests her. Hence, her other books are:

- **The Thinking Game:**
  A Winning Strategy for Achieving Your Goals

- **The Smart Woman's Guide to Style & Clothing:**
  A Step-by-Step Process for Creating the Perfect Wardrobe

- **From Photographer to Gallery Artist:**
  The Complete Guide to Finding Gallery Representation for Your Fine Art Photography

- **Simoni's Gift:**
  A Story about Your Purpose in Life

- **Wake Up to Powerful Living:**
  12 Principles to Transform Your Life

In addition to writing books, Kara Lane is a Financial Forensics Consultant, Certified Public Accountant (CPA), and Certified Fraud Examiner (CFE).

She grew up in Indianapolis and received her B.S. degree in Business from Indiana University. She majored in accounting and minored in communication, and still uses both skills. She lives in Carmel, Indiana, with her husband, Rick.

You can contact her at kara@karalane.com or through her website at https://www.karalane.com/. She'd love to hear from you. OK, enough of the third person...I would love to hear from you. While my *Crappy Advice for a Happy Life* book was obviously written tongue-in-cheek, I'm always curious to hear others' thoughts on happiness and life in general.

www.ingramcontent.com/pod-product-compliance
Lightning Source LLC
Chambersburg PA
CBHW011549070526
44585CB00023B/2522